InterActions
small group series

Finding God's
Strength
for Life's
Challenges

LIVING IN
GOD'S POWER

D1366985

Interactions Small Group Series

InterActions
small group series

Finding God's
Strength
for Life's
Challenges

LIVING IN
GOD'S POWER

Previously published as *Overcoming*

BILL HYBELS

WITH KEVIN AND SHERRY HARNEY

ZONDERVAN™

GRAND RAPIDS, MICHIGAN 49530 USA

WILLOW

Willow Creek Resources

ZONDERVAN™

Living in God's Power
Copyright © 1998 by Willow Creek Association
Previously published as *Overcoming*

Requests for information should be addressed to:

Zondervan, *Grand Rapids, Michigan 49530*

ISBN-10: 0-310-26606-8
ISBN-13: 978-0-310-26606-8

Interior design by Rick Devon and Michelle Espinoza

Printed in the United States of America

05 06 07 08 09 10 11 12 /❖ DCI/ 10 9 8 7 6 5 4 3 2 1

CONTENTS

INTERACTIONS

In 1992, Willow Creek Community Church, in partnership with Zondervan and the Willow Creek Association, released a curriculum for small groups entitled the Walking with God series. In just three years, almost a half million copies of these small group study guides were being used in churches around the world. The phenomenal response to this curriculum affirmed the need for relevant and biblical small group materials.

At the writing of this curriculum, there are nearly 3,000 small groups meeting regularly within the structure of Willow Creek Community Church. We believe this number will increase as we continue to place a central value on small groups. Many other churches throughout the world are growing in their commitment to small group ministries as well, so the need for resources is increasing.

In response to this great need, the Interactions small group series has been developed. Willow Creek Association and Zondervan have joined together to create a whole new approach to small group materials. These discussion guides are meant to challenge group members to a deeper level of sharing, create lines of accountability, move followers of Christ into action, and help group members become fully devoted followers of Christ.

SUGGESTIONS FOR INDIVIDUAL STUDY

1. Begin each session with prayer. Ask God to help you understand the passage and to apply it to your life.
2. A good modern translation, such as the New International Version, the New American Standard Bible, or the New Revised Standard Version, will give you the most help. Questions in this guide are based on the New International Version.
3. Read and reread the passage(s). You must know what the passage says before you can understand what it means and how it applies to you.
4. Write your answers in the spaces provided in the study guide. This will help you to express clearly your understanding of the passage.
5. Keep a Bible dictionary handy. Use it to look up unfamiliar words, names, or places.

SUGGESTIONS FOR GROUP STUDY

1. Come to the session prepared. Careful preparation will greatly enrich your time in group discussion.
2. Be willing to join in the discussion. The leader of the group will not be lecturing but will encourage people to discuss what they have learned in the passage. Plan to share what God has taught you in your individual study.
3. Stick to the passage being studied. Base your answers on the verses being discussed rather than on outside authorities such as commentaries or your favorite author or speaker.
4. Try to be sensitive to the other members of the group. Listen attentively when they speak, and be affirming whenever you can. This will encourage more hesitant members of the group to participate.
5. Be careful not to dominate the discussion. By all means participate, but allow others to have equal time.
6. If you are the discussion leader, you will find additional suggestions and helpful ideas in the Leader's Notes.

ADDITIONAL RESOURCES AND TEACHING MATERIALS

At the end of this study guide you will find a collection of resources and teaching materials to help you in your growth as a follower of Christ. You will also find resources that will help your church develop and build fully devoted followers of Christ.

INTRODUCTION: FINDING GOD'S STRENGTH FOR LIFE'S CHALLENGES

Every one of us faces moments of truth when we confront obstacles that could slow us down, trip us up, and seek to knock us out of the race. In these times we must to be overcomers—to live in victory rather than give in to defeat.

Your moment of truth might come when you see that uneasy look in your heart specialist's eyes at your annual checkup. It might hit you when your eighteen-year-old shouts, "I don't have to obey you anymore!" It might come as a flashback of some terrible injustice committed against you, or through the ever-present memory of that sin you just can't forgive yourself for or forget.

Adversity is the great leveler of the human race. It is no respecter of age, race, net worth, or spiritual delineation. We will all know hardship, loss, pressure, tragedy, heartbreak, and betrayal. If trouble hasn't reached you yet, it is probably coming.

Our reaction to adversity is quite predictable. Usually it begins with shock and utter disbelief: "I cannot believe this is happening to me. This kind of stuff only happens to other people." Then shock gives way to blaming. We tell ourselves, "This cannot be my fault." We start targeting blame against our boss, our spouse, our parents, or anyone else we can think of. Sometimes, if we can't blame others, we begin to target God.

At this point in the process we begin to withdraw, to find a dark, lonely place in which to hide out as blaming gives way to self-pity. As our pity festers, we become angry. We want someone to pay for what has happened to us. We lash out in an effort to get even. But getting even just leads to shame. We say, "What am I doing? This isn't helping. I've hurt innocent people with my thoughts and words and actions." Finally, the shame gives way to depression, despair, and utter defeat.

Just thinking about this process drives us to realize that there must be a way to overcome our troubles and meet adversity with courage instead of being ruled by our difficult circumstances. Jesus may have said we would face trouble in this life, but that was not the end of the story. He finished by saying, "But take heart! I have overcome the world" (John 16:33).

We don't have to cave in. We don't have to give up. Jesus wants us to know that He has overcome the adversities of this world and that He can teach us to become overcomers as well! He offers hope, help, and strength to overcome whatever you might be facing today.

Overcoming is about living a different way. It is about learning how, in God's strength, to overcome adversity, fear, apathy, greed, lust, sorrow, and all the things that can drag us down. This series of small group studies will be a powerful reminder that no matter what life hurls at us, no matter how badly we are treated, no matter how close to the edge of our endurance we get, with the power of Christ in us, we can be overcomers!

My prayer is that you will learn to tap into the power to become an overcomer—a remarkable power that is found in, and only in, the person of Jesus Christ.

Bill Hybels

OVERCOMING ADVERSITY

THE BIG PICTURE

Some years ago I heard a story of a fifty-six-year-old woman from Africa who faced adversity that most of us could barely imagine. Her nation was going through yet another famine, and she, in complete despondency, finally got a coupon from World Vision (a Christian relief agency) for a bag of rice. If she walked from her village to a feeding center in another city and traded the small piece of paper for a large bag of rice, she could probably stay alive for thirty days, until she had a chance to get another coupon.

The woman stood in line for much of the day and finally got her bag of rice. She walked around the city, and at one point, put her bag down to tend to something. She looked away for only a moment, but when she turned back, her bag of rice was gone—stolen. At that instant she realized that for the next thirty days she would face stomach-gnawing hunger and potential starvation. There would be no extra ticket or second bag of rice. To understand the full scope of this woman's suffering, you need to know that she had lost her husband and children in a previous famine. This is adversity beyond imagination.

We might not face famine, but adversity can come pounding down on us in many different ways. It is not much of an exaggeration to say that most of your small group members have felt or will feel the painful blow of adversity. It may come in the form of a financial, relational, or emotional beating. It may come from a stranger or from those closest to you. It may come slowly or out of the clear blue sky. But in the middle of our darkest moments, Jesus says, "Take courage. There is still hope. There is still a power that can sustain you during times of unbelievable tragedy and adversity." We all need to hear these words of encouragement.

A WIDE ANGLE VIEW

1 Choose *one* of the areas below and describe a time you faced adversity in that area:

- In the home
- In the marketplace
- In a friendship
- In the church
- In some other area of life

What helped you make it through this time?

A BIBLICAL PORTRAIT

Read Isaiah 43:1–3

2 In light of this passage, how would you respond to *each* of these statements:

If you live a good life and are faithful to God, you will never face suffering or adversity.

When I go through hard times, I have a feeling that
God has deserted me in my time of greatest need.

3 Isaiah speaks of "waters," "rivers," and "fire." What is
he talking about?

What is God doing while we are going through adversities?

*What are some of the "waters," "rivers," and "fires" you are
facing right now?*

SHARPENING THE FOCUS

Read Snapshot "What You Believe"

WHAT YOU BELIEVE

If we are going to overcome the adversities of this life, we must know what we believe. False beliefs can poison our thinking and weigh down our hearts. When facing the struggles of life, some basic beliefs must be firmly implanted in our minds or we are bound to get in trouble. Here are four essential beliefs for overcoming adversity:

1. God is not the author of evil. (James 1:12–18; Psalm 5:4)
2. God limits the severity of what we suffer and gives us power to overcome our adversity. (Philippians 4:13; 1 John 4:4; 1 Corinthians 10:13)
3. God is completely available in the middle of our troubles. He never leaves us alone to deal with them on our own. (Psalm 34:18; Psalm 23)
4. God is committed to bringing good out of the hardships of our lives. (Romans 8:28)

4

Why is each of these beliefs essential to overcoming adversity?

5

Take each belief and turn it around. If it was not true, what implications would this have on how we face adversity?

Read Snapshot "How You Grieve"

HOW YOU GRIEVE

If you are going to live as an overcomer, you have to know how to grieve. Some of us have never learned to allow ourselves to feel the deep and terrible sadness over the adversity we face. We don't feel free to tell God about it, to sob and weep over it, to cry until the tears run dry, and then to repeat the process as often as necessary.

Some of us lose sight of the fact that there is a tomorrow and there is a good God who rules over it. First Thessalonians 4:13 says some of us grieve as though there were no hope. But there is coming a day when there will be no more sadness, darkness, tragedy, or tears. There *is* hope as long as God is on the throne, as long as the resurrected Christ is available for relationship, and as long as the Holy Spirit lives inside of us. With this knowledge, we need to learn to grieve over the tragedies that have come our way, and then to move ahead with our lives.

6 Describe a time when you went through suffering and were able to grieve and pour your heart out to God.

How did the process of grieving help you heal?

7 Describe a time of struggle or adversity you have faced when you did not fully pour out your grief and sorrow.

What kept you from grieving?

Would you be willing to express your sorrow and grief about this adversity to your group?

Read Snapshot "Who You Lean On"

WHO YOU LEAN ON

Sometimes overcomers learn how to walk in victory when they find a few trusted friends they can lean on. When Jesus was drawing near the end of His life, He did not want to be alone. He took His three closest friends (Peter, James, and John) to a garden and asked them to keep watch with Him. He knew He was facing the cross and He needed a few friends around Him in His time of adversity. If Jesus needed people to lean on, who are we to think we can make it on our own?

---

8 What area of struggle or adversity have you been trying to face alone?

*How can your group members pray for you and offer you
support?*

9 Discuss a person who you are aware is going through
a time of adversity. What can you do as a small group
to offer practical help, encouragement, and support?

PUTTING YOURSELF IN THE PICTURE

DEEPENING BELIEF

Take time in the coming week to memorize and think deeply
about the following passages:

> I can do everything through him who gives me strength.
> > Philippians 4:13

> And we know that in all things God works for the good of
> those who love him, who have been called according to his
> purpose.
> > Romans 8:28

TIME FOR GRIEF

Commit to setting aside two half-hour sections of time in the coming week for dealing with unfinished grieving. Use this time to pour out your heart to God. Identify areas in which you still hold heartache and pain over adversity you have faced in your life. You may want to journal or to pray silently or out loud. Let any emotion surface that is within you; don't fear tears, anger, or frustration. God knows you inside and out and He can handle your emotions.

OVERCOMING FEAR

REFLECTIONS FROM SESSION 1

1. If you took time to memorize Philippians 4:13 and Romans 8:28, how are these portions of Scripture helping you overcome adversity?
2. If you fulfilled your commitment to spend two half-hour sections of time pouring out your heart to God, what feelings began to surface? Does this raise any prayer needs you would like to pass on to your group members?

THE BIG PICTURE

One of the most terrifying experiences of my whole life occurred in the auditorium of our church. It happened many years ago, when we were putting in a balcony. I was walking through the auditorium one day and saw the freshly laid I-beams suspended more than twenty feet in the air. I went up to check out the construction.

While I was up there, I was filled with this strange desire to see if I could walk across one of those ten-inch I-beams from the front all the way to the back without falling. I was halfway across the beam when a staff member came through the multi-purpose room. I think it was the look of horror on his face, but something made me realize what I was doing, and I started having an old-fashioned panic attack. I began to get short of breath, my pulse was racing, I became light-headed, and I couldn't move. Now, raw, blood-chilling fear is a bad feeling anywhere, but particularly troubling while trying to keep your balance on an I-beam more than twenty feet above the ground!

I'll tell you how this story ends later in the study.

A WIDE ANGLE VIEW

1 Describe a time when you faced intense fear.

A BIBLICAL PORTRAIT

Read Psalm 23 and 2 Timothy 1:7

2 What hope and encouragement does Psalm 23 offer to those who are facing fear?

3 In 2 Timothy 1:7 the apostle Paul draws a clear contrast between a *fearful* (timid) spirit and a *fearless* spirit. How does each of the following aspects of a fearless spirit help you become an overcomer?

- A spirit of power

- A spirit of love

- A spirit of self-discipline

SHARPENING THE FOCUS

Read Snapshot "Understanding the Origins of Our Fear"

UNDERSTANDING THE ORIGINS OF OUR FEAR

If we are serious about being liberated from fear, we must seek to understand fear's origin in our life. Dr. Joseph Wolpe, a South African psychiatrist who has spent most of his life helping people understand their phobias, was surprised to learn that many people live their entire lives tormented by a particular fear that developed from a single fright-filled event.

For example, if a teenager is dunked in a pool and held under the water until he feels he is going to drown, that single event could easily evolve into a lifelong fear of water, boats, pools, beaches, and any situation relating to water. In the same way, people who have a deep fear of public speaking can often remember someone laughing at them while they were giving an oral book report in class.

Only when we identify the birthplace of fear can we begin the process of overcoming it.

---

4 What are some common fears people face?

Where are the most likely breeding grounds for the birth of these fears?

5 Describe a fear you have overcome or one with which you still struggle. If you reflect, how do you think this fear was born?

Read Snapshot "Exposing the Lies"

EXPOSING THE LIES

Another step we must take if we are going to be serious about overcoming patterns of fear in our life is to expose fear's lies. In John 8:44, Jesus referred to the Evil One as a liar and the father of all lies. Jesus was exposing one of the devil's primary strategies for defeating followers of Christ—deception. The devil is a master at telling lies.

Imagine a man and a woman in a dating relationship. The woman tells the man, "I will call you tonight." The evening slowly passes and it is now midnight. There has been no call. Does fear prompt the man to think rational thoughts like, "Well, something probably came up. She had to work late or got busy helping out a friend. Or maybe she called when I was out running errands a little while ago." No! Fear would start spinning out nightmares: "I'll bet she is dead. She was in a horrible car accident and thrown from the car. I'll bet she was lying alone on the side of the road, her life ebbing away as she called my name, and I wasn't there for her." Or, "I'll bet she is dumping me! She said she cared, but now I am alone again."

Thoughts like these make for good soap opera story lines and country music lyrics, but they are not good for your emotional health. We need to expose such lies and say, "I will not become fearful over the lies of the Enemy. I will not be paralyzed by what might be."

6 What are some common lies the Enemy tells us in *one* of the following situations?

- If I don't find the right man or woman soon, I'll . . .
- If I don't get a raise, increase my standard of living, and move up in life, I'll . . .
- If I keep aging, keep getting more wrinkles, or keep losing my hair, I'll . . .
- If I become a follower of Christ and really live my life for Him, I'll . . .
- Create your own scenario:

7 What is one lie the Enemy is telling you right now?

How can your group members pray for you and help give you perspective as you seek to disarm this lie of the Enemy?

Read Snapshot "Declaring the Truth"

DECLARING THE TRUTH

Many scholars and researchers on fear management tell people to speak out against the lies the Enemy throws at them. Just say, "Stop these lies. Stop manufacturing and believing worse-case scenarios. Stop believing that you can't push back panicky feelings with the power of Christ."

Let's go back up to the ten-inch I-beam where I was standing paralyzed and in a cold sweat. That day I just said, "Stop!" I told myself the truth about the situation, the truth about my own abilities, the truth about God's willingness to help me out of this situation. I told myself, "If there was a ten-inch-wide line on the ground, I could walk on it for a mile with no problem. I can handle this." My pulse began to go down, I regained my equilibrium, and I walked slowly but surely across to the other side.

Winston Churchill used to say that if a person turned his back on fear, hoping that by avoiding it, it would go away, the fear would double and keep gaining strength. He also said that if the fear was faced promptly and directly, its power would be cut in half. Exposing the lies and speaking the truth is the best way to face fear head on!

---

8 Write down one area of fear in your life and the lies that accompany this fear:

The area of fear:

The lies of the Enemy:

Read these to your small group and invite them to speak God's truth to you in this area of fear.

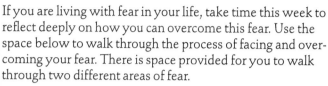

PUTTING YOURSELF IN THE PICTURE

Fear Assessment

If you are living with fear in your life, take time this week to reflect deeply on how you can overcome this fear. Use the space below to walk through the process of facing and overcoming your fear. There is space provided for you to walk through two different areas of fear.

The area of fear:

The origins of this fear:

The lies the Enemy is telling me that cause deeper fear:

The truth of God I need to speak against the Enemy and my fear:

One person who can pray for me and support me as I face my fear:

The area of fear:

The origins of this fear:

The lies the Enemy is telling me that cause deeper fear:

The truth of God I need to speak against the Enemy and my fear:

One person who can pray for me and support me as I face my fear:

OVERCOMING APATHY

REFLECTIONS FROM SESSION 2

1. If you took time to do an assessment of fear in your life, what did you discover about the origin of your fear?
2. What is one truth you are speaking to fight against this fear?

THE BIG PICTURE

Thousands of children die every day of starvation and diseases caused by malnutrition. Over one billion people in this world live at subsistence level with regard to food, shelter, and clothing. Sadly, the situation just seems to be getting worse.

While these statistics are mind-numbing, too often we think in terms of numbers and statistics rather than real people. However, on a trip to the Dominican Republic, these statistics became very real to me. One mother I met there had grown up in a 12 x 12 foot shanty with a thatch roof and cardboard walls. When she got a little older and married, she and her husband could not afford to live anyplace else, so her family hung a sheet over one little corner of the little shanty and that become her new residency.

Over time this woman and her husband had three little girls. Somewhere along the line, her husband deserted her and the girls. Now raising her girls alone, most of the woman's day was consumed with trying to find food to feed them. She continued to live behind the sheet in her parents' shanty, doing her best to provide for her family in circumstances most of us could not begin to imagine.

As I stood in the little shanty talking with this woman, one of the little girls was waking up from a nap. I remembered the way I would greet my daughter after she woke up from a nap when she was a little girl. I rubbed the little girl's hands and spoke softly to her, as I had to my own daughter countless times. In that moment, as I moved closer to her and reached out to touch her, that little girl was no longer a statistic; instead, she was not much different than my daughter, a child for whom Christ died. She was a little one who matters to God.

Through this encounter, I discovered that if I want to put apathy and self-indulgence to death, I need to get face-to-face with those who are hurting. If we are going to overcome apathy, we need to allow ourselves to feel the pain of others and take some kind of meaningful action. I am reminded of a story I heard some years ago that bears out this message in a simple, yet clear way:

> There was a ten-year-old boy who went to the beach the morning after a huge tropical storm. There were thousands upon thousands of starfish lying on the shore, dying. This little kid felt bad for the helpless starfish, so one by one he was picking them up and throwing them back into the ocean. A practical, cynical older gentleman came along and saw this little guy doing all he could to save a few starfish. He said to the boy, "Do you really think you are going to make any difference with all these thousands and thousands of starfish? Do you really think what you are doing makes any difference at all?" The little kid happened to be holding a starfish at the moment. He held it up and responded, "Well, I am pretty sure I am making a difference to this one." And with that, he hurled the starfish back into the safety of the water.

A WIDE ANGLE VIEW

1 Describe a time you felt like the little boy in the starfish story.

Describe a time you felt like the older gentleman in the story and wondered if your "little contribution" to the world's problems really made any difference at all.

A BIBLICAL PORTRAIT

Read Luke 10:25–37

2 What do you learn about apathy from this story?

3 The Samaritan in this story had the antidote to apathy. What do you see in his *attitudes* and *actions* that challenge you to overcome apathy?

Read Snapshot "Using Your Heart"

USING YOUR HEART

In my encounter with the woman and her three daughters in the Dominican Republic, I discovered that the first step to overcoming apathy was allowing my heart to be touched. Like the Good Samaritan, we need to allow ourselves to feel pity. Like the little boy trying to save the starfish, we have to care enough to try to make a difference. When our hearts are broken with the pain of others, we begin to see them as people loved by God. Until we get close enough for our hearts to be touched, we will remain calloused and removed . . . apathetic!

4 World Vision has a motto: "Let your heart be broken by the things that break the heart of God." Describe a time this happened to you.

5 What is one area in which you are experiencing a broken heart for the needs of others?

What is one area in which you feel your heart is calloused and needs to be broken?

Read Snapshot "Using Your Head"

USING YOUR HEAD

Allowing your heart to be broken is a first step, but it's not enough. If you stop there, you might feel badly or shed a few tears, but nothing happens. Next, you need to use your head to create a strategy for making a difference. The Good Samaritan had a clear plan of action in mind that would help the injured man with his immediate as well as ongoing needs. The boy with a tender heart for starfish planned to throw as many back into the water as his little hands could carry. At Willow Creek Community Church, we continue to strategize and make practical plans for how we can help families in the Dominican Republic (as well as other places of need across the globe). You must have a clear, intelligent plan of action if you are going to overcome apathy.

6 What plans and strategies has your church established to help meet the needs of others in your community and around the world?

If your church is strong in this department, take time to lift up prayers of praise as well as prayers for effectiveness in these ministries.

If your church is weak in this area, pray for God to breathe new vision into your church and pray for apathy to be driven out.

7 What are some of the things followers of Christ can do in order to make a difference in the life of someone in need?

Read Snapshot "Using Your Hands"

USING YOUR HANDS

When you allow yourself to get close to those who are hurting and suffering, your apathy begins to erode. Suddenly, your heart becomes tender and you begin to feel, to hurt, to care. Next, you use your head to strategize how you can make a difference. But tender hearts and good intentions are not enough. You need to move into action.

The Good Samaritan paid a price when he stopped to help a bloody and broken traveler on the road. It cost him time, energy, physical strength, and money out of his pocket! He got his hands dirty, and probably ended up with some blood on his robe. The little boy along the seashore threw starfish back into the ocean until his little fingers were raw and his arms were sore. Our church continues to send money, supplies, and people into mission fields like the Dominican Republic. The final blow to apathy is always action. When our hands are busy helping heal the hurts of others, we no longer have time to be apathetic.

8

What obstacles tend to stand in the way of you moving into action and meeting the needs of those who are hurting?

9

What is one action goal you need to set that involves getting your hands busy serving others in *one* of these areas:

- In your home
- In your church
- In your community
- In your world

An Action Plan for Defeating Apathy

Apathy is sent running for the door when we have tender hearts, conceive a clear plan, and begin moving into action on behalf of our Lord. Identify one place in your life where you want to strategize how you can move into action. Use this basic outline as you develop a plan for overcoming apathy:

In what area are you sensing apathy in your life?

How can you get yourself closer to this situation or place of need so that God can begin to soften your heart?

What specific strategy can you develop to prepare yourself to make a difference in this area of need?

What are the practical actions you will take to get your hands moving and serving those who are in need?

OVERCOMING GREED

REFLECTIONS FROM SESSION 3

1. How has your heart been softening and becoming less apathetic in one specific area?
2. What is one action you have taken since your last small group to deal a blow to apathy?

THE BIG PICTURE

Have you ever heard of a "Price Tag Moment"? This is when you find something you really like at a store and you start getting excited about the idea of that item becoming yours. You just love it! You want it! You must have it! However, one final hurdle has to be crossed. You reach slowly toward the little tag that will tell you the rest of the story, turning it slowly until your eyes fall on the series of numbers. That moment, when you see the price and let your mind soak it in, is a price tag moment!

Sometimes the price of that most-wanted object is cause for great joy, excitement, and relief, but most of the time seeing the price moves you directly from the price tag moment to sticker shock! Now you have a decision to make: to buy or not to buy.

I was traveling some years ago in a city that was much colder than I had thought it was going to be. I hadn't brought a coat, so I went downtown to do a little shopping. I found a clothing store with a big orange "SALE" sign in the front window, so I went in and made a beeline for the coatrack. I found a coat I liked and glanced at the price tag. It was one of those rare positive price tag moments—the coat was only $79. As I headed to the front of the store I thought, *I'm going to come back to this store and do some real shopping some day. I love a good sale!*

I found a salesclerk to check me out so I could get back on the road. She looked at my new coat and said, with a sort of European flair, "Exquisite selection, sir." This should have told me was in trouble. She rang up my sale coat and to my shock, the register said $790.00! I started getting chest pains!

I quickly ran back and put the coat on the rack and said, "Stay there. You can rot and die before I'll pay that kind of money. Get away from me." As I left the store, I asked the salesclerk if there was a less "exquisite" store in the area.

I will never forget that price tag moment.

A WIDE ANGLE VIEW

1 Describe one of your most memorable price tag moments.

A BIBLICAL PORTRAIT

Read Luke 18:18–30

2 What was this man seeking to buy and what was the price tag?

How did this become his ultimate price tag moment?

3 What do you learn about the heart of the ruler in the story?

What do you learn about the power of riches?

What do you learn about the heart of Jesus?

SHARPENING THE FOCUS

Read Snapshot "Acknowledging the Reality of Greed"

ACKNOWLEDGING THE REALITY OF GREED

How do you overcome greed? If you are serious about overcoming greed and living free from its claws, the first thing you have to do is acknowledge its reality. Do not say you are exempt from its pull and power; face it, greed affects all of us to one degree or another. When you notice your eyes wandering toward all that glitters and your heart hungering for more, more, more . . . admit it! Then pray for wisdom to discern what is a normal, healthy desire and what grows from the sinister drive of old-fashioned greed.

The second thing to do is to learn to bring your struggle with greed out into the open. Get with a small group of people who love you and who are willing to speak the truth to you. When you are thinking about a bigger house, a new car, a job change, some extra way of earning income, or a new "toy," communicate your plans to this group. Ask them, "Does this seem like a healthy, God-honoring desire or does it seem greed-driven? Ultimately, you will make the decision, but the counsel of other Christ followers brings a wealth of perspective when you are seeking to overcome greed.

4 What is an area of greed you have battled and in which you have experienced victory?

What helped you say no to the seduction of greed in this area of your life?

5

In your small group, you are in a great setting to do just what is encouraged in the Snapshot above. What one big purchase or financial move are you considering making? Communicate this to your group and invite them to help you gain perspective on what is driving this desire.

Read Snapshot "Exposing Greed's Lies"

EXPOSING GREED'S LIES

Another thing to do to overcome greed is to expose its lies. So much of greed's power exists in its exaggerations, deceptions, and lies! The Evil One whispers in our ears with that greedy little voice, "Just twenty percent more income and you will be happy! A little nicer this. A little more of that. Something a little grander, bigger, faster, or newer and your life will be healthy, happy, and wonderful beyond belief." He whispers the lie of lies, "Happiness is dictated by what you have!" The sad reality is, too many of us have believed the lie.

I was talking with a friend who told me he earned fifty percent less this year than he did last year. I asked, "How do you feel about that?" He answered, "Well, it has kind of made me do a reality check. But, in all honesty, I still have more than I need. Now, when I hear that little voice say, 'Work until you drop. Get more, more, more. Don't worry about being there for your family,' I just have to remind myself that more isn't always the answer." Here is a guy who is learning to expose the lie of greed, and it is setting him free!

Greed is the proverbial carrot on the stick. The harder we work to arrive at happiness through the accumulation of things, the *less* happy we become. The faster we run and the harder we work, the *less* satisfaction we feel. No matter what we do, the carrot is always just beyond our reach. We need to expose the lie of greed and realize that material things will never satisfy.

6 Identify the sources that perpetuate the greed lie. Finish *one* of these statements:

- The message of commercials feed the greed lie by telling me . . .
- The heartbeat and pulse of the business world fuel the greed lie by driving me to . . .
- Seeking the "American Dream" can encourage greed by . . .

G

7 What are some of the lies behind these statements? Choose one and respond:

- If I could get the promotion and pay increase I have been working for, I would finally be able to slow down my frenzied work pace and be content with my financial situation.
- If we could build our own house and have the space we really need, I would never complain again.
- If we could get a nice ski boat [or some other toy], we could pull our family together around this new recreational opportunity. It would be the key to happiness among our children.

Read Snapshot "God's Program for Overcoming Greed"

GOD'S PROGRAM FOR OVERCOMING GREED

If you really want to tame greed, you had better order your financial affairs according to God's wisdom and Word. God's program for property management calls us to do a number of things that are simple to understand, but not always simple to do.

First, you need to *earn money according to your potential*—not less or more. The push to do more than we can handle drives us into the arms of greed. Second, you need to *enjoy the fruit of your labor.* Give thanks to God and enjoy what He provides. Too many people spend their whole life making more and more and never enjoying what they have. Third, learn to *live well within your means.* Spend considerably less than you earn. Form a game plan. Avoid destructive debt patterns. Set savings aside on a consistent basis so you can live free from the destructive power of debt. Fourth, *give a percentage of your earnings consistently to God's work.* God's program for property management calls all Christ followers to give ten percent (a tithe) to support God's work on this earth. Every time you do this you are acknowledging God's rule over your personal finances. Fifth, *seek guidance from God on a regular basis* for promptings regarding money management. Beyond the ten percent you give on a regular basis, God will open doors for you to use your resources to help others and further His work.

8 Which of these five guidelines do you find easiest to follow?

What has helped you develop this practice in your life?

9 Which of these five guidelines do you find most difficult to incorporate into your life?

How can your group members support you as you learn to develop in this area of your life?

PUTTING YOURSELF IN THE PICTURE

LETTING GOD'S WORD EXPOSE THE GREED-LIE

Take time in the coming days to read, reflect on, and memorize this passage:

> But godliness with contentment is great gain. For we brought nothing into the world, and we can take nothing out of it. But if we have food and clothing, we will be content with that. People who want to get rich fall into temptation and a trap and into many foolish and harmful desires that plunge men into ruin and destruction. For the love of money is a root of all kinds of evil. Some people, eager for money, have wandered from the faith and pierced themselves with many griefs.
>
> 1 Timothy 6:6–10

GREED AND THE NEXT GENERATION

Too often we pass down our weaknesses from generation to generation. In the coming month, meet with one person who is younger than you and teach that person what you learned from this study. Communicate what you have learned, how you have been challenged, and even where you have been convicted of greed in your life. Allow God to use you to help cut off the generational curse of greed.

OVERCOMING LUST

REFLECTIONS FROM SESSION 4

1. If you took time to memorize 1 Timothy 6:6–10, would you quote some or all of this passage for your small group? How has this passage helped you expose some of the lies surrounding greed?

2. If you took time to meet with a person younger than you to communicate what you have learned about overcoming greed, tell your group about this meeting.

THE BIG PICTURE

In your mind, transport yourself to the home where you grew up. Think about your most vivid memories of Christmas. Can you see where the Christmas tree was in the house? What did the Christmas tree look like? Where did your dad usually sit? How about your mom? Where were your siblings? Did you open your presents on Christmas Eve or on Christmas Day? What images fill your mind and what feelings fill your heart?

Now transport yourself to your favorite vacation spot. Maybe you are on a beach, maybe in the mountains, maybe on a lush green golf course. Maybe you have a mental picture of a quiet lake or the sun-drenched deck of a boat. Allow your mind to fill with all the details of this place—the colors, the sounds, even the smells. There are feelings that come with this place because you have been there with people you love.

Now focus back on the here and now. The human imagination is pretty amazing, isn't it! Without travel hassles or expense you can instantaneously transport yourself incredible distances.

With the power of imagination we can picture ourselves and others in all kinds of settings. We can picture what we would like to be doing ten years from now in our vocational life or maybe even in our retirement years. Leaders of organizations put their imaginations and prayers together to try to figure out where a company or a church is going to be five years from now. And even more exciting, with our God-given power of imagination we can hang on to our hope of heaven and picture ourselves finally free from the struggles and heartaches of this life. The human ability to imagine is an awesome gift from God and we should thank Him often for the joy it can bring.

A WIDE ANGLE VIEW

1 Finish one of these statements:

- When I imagined Christmas from my childhood, some of the images and feelings were . . .
- When I imagined my favorite vacation spot, some of the images and feelings were . . .

A BIBLICAL PORTRAIT

Read Matthew 5:27–30

2 Our imagination is a great gift from God. However, it has a shadow side. Not only can we imagine things that are God-honoring, but we can imagine things that break the heart of the God we love. What does this passage teach you about the shadow side of our human imagination?

How does God feel about a person using his or her imagination to exploit another person by lusting?

3 A hyperbole is an exaggeration used to make a point. What hyperbole does Jesus use in this passage, and what is the message Jesus is seeking to communicate through such extreme statements?

SHARPENING THE FOCUS

Read Snapshot "Two Foundational Questions"

TWO FOUNDATIONAL QUESTIONS

In order to overcome lust, there are two basic questions we need to ask: "What is lust?" and "Why is lust so destructive?"

In answering the first question I would say that lust is taking a complete, complex human being, made in the image of God, and reducing him or her to just a body dedicated to the gratification of the luster's sexual desires. A person caught up in lust doesn't care about the other person's thoughts, feelings, spiritual condition, worries, anxieties, or aspirations. Lust is fundamentally self-seeking and completely devoid of love.

In response to the second question, regarding why lust is so destructive, I would invite you to reflect on the words of a letter I received from a man caught up into the vicious cycle of lusting:

Dear Bill,

I am an emotional invalid. Lust is eating me up. It paralyzes my spiritual life, it perverts my view of the world, it distorts my social life, it wreaks havoc in my emotional stability, it destroys any possibility of God using me fully, and I just can't stop. Recently I have become addicted to pornography, which is just intensifying my problem. The sad part is that I know that lust and pornography promise everything but produce nothing, and I still just can't stop. Please, somebody, help me.

4 According to the definition of lusting in the Snapshot, what does lusting do to another human being?

How would it feel to discover that someone was using you in this way?

5 How does lusting hurt:

- The one who lusts?

- The one who is used as the object of lust?

- The heart of God?

- Our society?

Read Snapshot "Levels of Lusting"

LEVELS OF LUSTING

Level-one lusters are best described as those people who infrequently and almost accidentally lust. These are folks for whom lust is basically a nonissue except for the occasional surprise jolt that temporarily upsets their mental apple cart. They might receive that jolt from watching a particular movie or TV show, or it might be that they begin thinking of a colleague or a neighbor in a more sexual way than they had in the past. This type of lust is involuntary and rarely the cause of deep shame or guilt. Thoughts come to mind, but they are not dwelt on. Instead, they are quickly confessed to God, forgiveness is received, and these people move on without much stumbling in this area of their life.

Level-two lusters know they wrestle a lot with lustful thoughts. They take lustful thoughts all the way to the end in their mind, creating sexual scenarios and playing them over and over and over in living Technicolor. They may have viewed a little pornography here and there, and they may have rented some videos they wouldn't want others to know about. They might even have visited adult bookstores, surfed the Internet, or dialed up a 900 number seeking new fuel to feed their lust. Sometimes level-two lusters go through seasons where lusting isn't that big of an issue; at other times it is about the only thing they can think about. Because of the power of lust during these times, they are often racked by guilt and shame.

Level-three lusters are consumed by their lust. In his book *Out of the Shadows*, Dr. Patrick Karns says that, at a certain point in time, sexual preoccupation becomes a person's reason for being. It is their remedy for pain, their reward for success, their means for maintaining emotional balance. There is an ongoing tension between the person's normal self and the addicted self. A Jekyll-and-Hyde struggle emerges and the power of lust begins to be so compelling that to stop the pattern would feel like dying. A level-three luster begins to arrange his or her life around participation in this secret life, a life filled with thought patterns, videos, phone calls, magazines, bars, and bookstore rendezvous that get increasingly risky and expensive.

6 What do you see in our culture that feeds lust and pushes a person from level one to level two to level three?

7 How do men and women differ when it comes to the battle with lusting?

Read Snapshot "Instructions for Overcoming Lust"

INSTRUCTIONS FOR OVERCOMING LUST

There is no simple three-step program for overcoming lust. However, there are some basic guidelines that will help a person as he or she seeks to break the cycle of lusting. I'd like to suggest four helpful instructions for a person who desires to overcome lust.

First, *own up!* Admit you have a problem. No more excuses, rationalizations, and cover-ups. Simply say, "I have a problem with lusting!" In 1 John 1:9 we are told that forgiveness begins when we confess our sins.

Second, *dig in!* Dr. Karns points out four false beliefs that pervert our view of the world and push a person toward a pattern of lusting:

1. I am a bad, unworthy person.
2. No one could ever love me the way I am.
3. My needs will never be met.
4. Sex is the most important need in my life.

Take time to dig into your own heart and see if these feelings ring true for you. If they do, you may need a Christian counselor to help sort out where they come from and how they can be removed from your view of life.

Third, *reach out!* Lust, by its very nature, lures a person into a dark, secretive, lonely existence. Recovery from lust will happen only as people come out of hiding, share their secret, and expose their problem in the light of community. Sometimes this happens with one or two close friends; at other times it can happen among a group of trusted friends. But reaching out is essential in the process of overcoming lust.

Fourth, *pitch in!* Lust, especially at levels two and three, consumes an enormous amount of time and energy. When you are on the recovery road, you will discover you have time and energy that needs to be invested in something else. In Luke 11 Jesus taught that if you clean a bunch of junk out of a house (symbolic of a human heart), the removal of the junk leaves a vacuum. If you don't fill this space with good stuff, the evil might come back and multiply. As you battle lust, fill the time and energy vacuum in your life with meaningful service in the church and world. Rather than using people as objects to satisfy your lust, spend your time serving and building people up.

8 What do you believe God would say to a person who believed the lies listed below? Respond to *one*:

- I am a bad, unworthy person.
- No one could ever love me the way I am.
- My needs will never be met.
- Sex is the most important need in my life.

9

What are some practical ways that we can cut off the sources of lust-producing images?

What are some practical ways that we can keep ourselves from situations that might encourage lusting?

How could your small group, or individual relationships in your small group, function as a place for support and help in the battle against lust?

PUTTING YOURSELF IN THE PICTURE

AN HONEST LOOK AT YOUR LIFE:

To overcome lust, we must first admit we are in a battle. Take time in the coming week to reflect on your life. Use the questions below to guide you.

How much time in a week do you spend in sexual fantasy?

What kind of visual images do you feed into your mind through movies, TV, magazines, the Internet and other sources of visual stimulation?

What kind of thoughts do you allow into your heart through books, magazine articles, phone conversations, and other sources of mental pictures?

How often do you look at a person in an exclusively sexual way?

In complete honesty, between you and God, are you a level-one, level-two or level- three luster? Confess this to God and seek His help as you begin the process of owning up, digging in, reaching out, and pitching in.

A TIME FOR HOUSECLEANING

If you are going to get serious about overcoming lust, you may need to do some serious housecleaning. This could mean throwing out magazines, videos, and any other materials in your home that are sexually explicit. It could also mean canceling your cable (or specific channels) and Internet service (or having a block placed on all sexually explicit materials). If you travel for business and spend a lot of time in hotels, ask for a block to be placed on any channels that might bring pornography into your room. If a hotel can't do this, and you are a level-two or three luster, don't even go into the room—find another hotel. Jesus taught that lust was so serious we should be willing to cut off any source that encourages it.

OVERCOMING SORROW

REFLECTIONS FROM SESSION 5

*Please note that these reflections from session five might be discussed as a group or one-on-one with another group member.

1. If you took time to look honestly at the place of lust in your life, what is one prayer need you would like to bring to your small group or to one member of your small group?

2. If you took time to look honestly at the place of lust in your life, what is one area in which you need someone to encourage you and keep you accountable to keep resisting the temptations of lust?

THE BIG PICTURE

Some years ago I ran across a book by John James and Frank Cherry about grief recovery. In this book, they tell the story of a fictional boy to whom they give the name Johnny. Their goal is to illustrate the conventional approach to sorrow management. This is a summary of their story:

When Johnny is five years old, his dog suddenly dies. Johnny is stunned, and cries for hours. The dog had been his constant companion, had slept at the foot of his bed, and now he is dead. Johnny's parents are caught off guard by Johnny's deeply emotional response and they scramble for ways to relieve Johnny's pain. Finally his dad says, "Don't feel bad, Johnny. Saturday we will get you a new dog."

A few years later Johnny's bike is stolen. Again his dad says, "Shake it off, buddy, we will get you a new one." Later on, when Johnny is in high school, he falls in love with a freshman. The world has never looked brighter . . . until she dumps him unceremoniously. All of a sudden a curtain covers the sun. Johnny is heartbroken. This time it is not just a puppy or a ten-speed that can be replaced at the local store. Mom comes to the rescue and says, with great sensitivity, "Don't feel bad, Johnny, there are other fish in the sea."

Some years later, John's grandfather dies. He and John had fished together every summer and were very close. John actually found out about his grandfather's death when someone slipped him a note in math class. He read the words on the paper and started getting misty-eyed. Then, without warning he started to sob openly at his desk. It was a rather awkward situation, so the teacher excused him and sent him to the school office where he could be alone. When his father picked him up and brought him home, he saw his mother weeping in the living room and he wanted to run and embrace her, but his dad said, "Don't disturb her. She needs to be alone. She will be all right in a little while." So John goes to his room and cries alone. He feels a deeper sense of loneliness than he has ever known.

In an effort to "be strong" John buries his feelings and replaces his sense of loss with a host of activities at school and in the neighborhood. Even with all his effort to forget and move on, John still finds himself thinking about his grandfather constantly. His mind keeps going back to fishing trips, Christmas Eves, birthday parties, and other special moments. This preoccupation continues on for months until he finally tells his dad about it. His father says, "Just give it some more time and everything will be fine."

So John gives it time, lots of time, but his sorrow does not seem to go away. What makes matters worse is that, as he remembers the details of his relationship with his grandfather, John realizes he had never really thanked him for the fishing trips, the sack lunches, the afternoon swims, and all the fun times they enjoyed together. In fact, he realizes that he had never even told his grandfather that he loved him. He had left so many things unsaid! And now it is too late. He comes to the conclusion that he would have to live with regret for the rest of his life.

With all the inner turmoil John is facing, he says to himself, "Close relationships are just too painful. I am going to back off from any deep involvement in other relationships." John decides that he will protect himself from future sorrow by building a wall around his heart and life. He will wise up, toughen up, and avoid future sorrow. He has gotten his diploma from the school of hard knocks and he has learned his lesson well.

A WIDE ANGLE VIEW

1 What messages did Johnny receive about suffering and grief as he was growing up?

What messages did you receive about how to deal with grief as you were growing up?

A BIBLICAL PORTRAIT

Read John 11:32–44 and Psalm 116:1–9

2 From John 11:32–44, what do you learn about how Jesus dealt with sorrow?

3 In Psalm 116 the writer is in the midst of sorrow and struggle. What do you learn about how the psalmist dealt with his sorrow in this passage?

What can a person in the midst of sorrow learn about God from this psalm?

SHARPENING THE FOCUS

Read Snapshot "Conventional Wisdom on Sorrow Management"

CONVENTIONAL WISDOM ON SORROW MANAGEMENT

The authors I mentioned in the "Big Picture" section of this study highlight at least six elements to the conventional wisdom on sorrow management. They are:

1. *Bury your feelings.* If you are hurting, stuff it down. Be sure you don't complicate things and make all your relationships messy with all your sorrow, tears, and emotional turmoil.
2. *Replace your loss as soon as possible.* Turn the page. Fix it quick. Move on. You can deal with your sorrow by getting that new dog, buying a new bike, or finding a new girlfriend.
3. *Grieve alone. When you are in the throws of sorrow, don't drag everyone else down with you.* Pull yourself together, and when you are with others, grin and bear it.
4. *Time will heal your sorrow.* Time has a mystical power to magically heal all ills. Just wait and see, everything will be better.
5. *Learn to live with regret.* Often there is nothing you can do to go back and make things right. Just expect to carry regret and disappointment for the rest of your life.
6. *Once burned, twice smart.* Once you have felt the pain of life, you will learn to buffer yourself. If you are wise, you will put up the necessary defenses and be sure you don't get hurt again.

4 How can the conventional wisdom on sorrow management be counter-productive to the healing process?

5 Suppose you have a close friend who has just lost a
very close family member. How would you respond to
one of these statements made by your friend:

- I just need to get away from everyone and everything until I can pull myself together. I really don't
want to interact with anyone until I have my act
together.
- I'm just trying to focus on what I have. There is no
use in dwelling on what I have lost.
- I guess I'll just have to wait until my heart heals
itself. I suppose in a few months everything will be
back to normal.

6 If you have been raised on the conventional wisdom
for grief management, what are you learning about the
error of these thought patterns?

How can your small group members pray for you and support you as you seek to uncover where you have adopted the conventional wisdom in your approach to dealing with grief?

Read Snapshot "God's Wisdom on Sorrow Management"

GOD'S WISDOM ON SORROW MANAGEMENT

For each of the unhealthy elements of the conventional wisdom on sorrow management, God has an antidote. God's wisdom for sorrow management is counter-cultural. When facing sorrow, God's wisdom says:

1. *Be open with your grief.* We grieve as those who have a hope that can never be taken away (1 Thess. 4:13). We have hope in Christ and the promise of heaven. Jesus openly showed His sorrow; we should learn from His example.

2. *Review your loss.* Don't try to replace your loss immediately; instead, reflect deeply and allow yourself to feel the fullness of the loss.

3. *Grieve in community.* God's plan was never for us to go through times of sorrow alone. We need to be in community and draw from the love and strength of others (Rom. 12:15; 1 Cor. 12:26).

4. *The Holy Spirit of God heals hearts, not time alone.* God, by His Spirit, is our Comforter and Counselor. We need to seek Him in the healing process (2 Cor. 1:3–4).

5. *Realize you don't have to carry regret for the rest of your life.* God can lift the load of regret and guilt. He is the God of new beginnings.

6. *As Christ followers, we never lose our ultimate treasure.* Although this life can deal us some harsh blows, Jesus Christ is our ultimate treasure. Nothing can take Him away. With this in mind, we don't need to get cynical and hardhearted.

7

How does God's plan for sorrow management fly in the face of conventional wisdom?

Why are these two systems so radically different?

8 Is there a point of sorrow in your life that you have been burying instead of communicating openly? Take time to tell your group members about this area of sorrow.

How can your group members pray for you and be an encouragement to you as you overcome sorrow in this area of your life?

PUTTING YOURSELF IN THE PICTURE

SOME "TO DO'S"

In her book *Helping People Through Grief,* Delores Kuning talks about how to care for others who are going through a time of sorrow. Here is a summary of some of her observations:

1. *Acknowledge the loss.* Stop by and extend care. Don't ignore the pain someone is facing. You might stumble and bumble your way through it, but don't let somebody go through a season of loss without your acknowledging it.
2. *Give the mourner permission to grieve* and express his or her emotions.
3. *Free the grief-stricken person to talk about his loss.* Those in mourning reflect on their loss often, and they will want to talk about those feelings. Provide opportunity for honest conversation.
4. *Offer practical forms of help*: meals, child care, transportation, etc. Exact needs vary from person to person, but there are always practical ways you can help.
5. *Follow up monthly for the first year.* Most of us tend to fade too quickly when others experience a loss. Commit to making a phone call, sending a note, or dropping by every month for a year. Be part of people's healing for the long haul.

Commit to using some of these practical "to do" tools as you walk with others through their times of sorrow.

WATCH WHAT YOU SAY

There are some things we should avoid saying when others are going through loss and sorrow. Don't make careless statements like: "It was God's will," "He is better off now," "She had a full life," or "I understand how you feel." When people are suffering, they don't need your advice or wisdom; they need your love. If you must say something, "I am so sorry over the loss you have experienced" would be a safe place to start. But don't try to defend God or explain people's pain. Often, sitting with them in silence or sharing a warm embrace says more than a thousand words.

Leader's Notes

eading a Bible discussion—especially for the first time—can make you feel both nervous and excited. If you are nervous, realize that you are in good company. Many biblical leaders, uch as Moses, Joshua, and the apostle Paul, felt nervous and nadequate to lead others (see, for example, 1 Cor. 2:3). Yet God's grace was sufficient for them, just as it will be for you.

ome excitement is also natural. Your leadership is a gift to he others in the group. Keep in mind, however, that other roup members also share responsibility for the group. Your ole is simply to stimulate discussion by asking questions and ncouraging people to respond. The suggestions listed below an help you to be an effective leader.

Preparing to Lead

1. Ask God to help you understand and apply the passage to your own life. Unless that happens, you will not be prepared to lead others.
2. Carefully work through each question in the study guide. Meditate and reflect on the passage as you formulate your answers.
3. Familiarize yourself with the Leader's Notes for each session. These will help you understand the purpose of the session and will provide valuable information about the questions in the session. The Leader's Notes are not intended to be read to the group. These notes are primarily for your use as a group leader and for your preparation. However, when you find a section that relates well to your group, you may want to read a brief portion or encourage them to read this section at another time.
4. Pray for the various members of the group. Ask God to use these sessions to make you better disciples of Jesus Christ.
5. Before the first session, make sure each person has a study guide. Encourage them to prepare beforehand for each session.

Leading the Session

1. Begin the session on time. If people realize that the session begins on schedule, they will work harder to arrive on time.

2. At the beginning of your first time together, explain that these sessions are designed to be discussions, not lectures. Encourage everyone to participate, but realize some may be hesitant to speak during the first few sessions.

3. Don't be afraid of silence. People in the group may need time to think before responding.

4. Avoid answering your own questions. If necessary, rephrase a question until it is clearly understood. Even an eager group will quickly become passive and silent if they think the leader will do most of the talking.

5. Encourage more than one answer to each question. Ask, "What do the rest of you think?" or "Anyone else?" until several people have had a chance to respond.

6. Try to be affirming whenever possible. Let people know you appreciate their insights into the passage.

7. Never reject an answer. If it is clearly wrong, ask, "Which verse led you to that conclusion?" Or let the group handle the problem by asking them what they think about the question.

8. Avoid going off on tangents. If people wander off course gently bring them back to the passage being considered.

9. Conclude your time together with conversational prayer. Ask God to help you apply those things that you learned in the session.

10. End on time. This will be easier if you control the pace of the discussion by not spending too much time on some questions or too little on others.

We encourage all small group leaders to use *Leading Life-Changing Small Groups* (Zondervan) by Bill Donahue and the Willow Creek Small Group Team while leading their group. Developed and used by Willow Creek Community Church, this guide is an excellent resource for training and equipping followers of Christ to effectively lead small groups. It includes valuable information on how to utilize fun and creative relationship-building exercises for your group; how to plan your meeting; how to share the leadership load by identifying, developing, and working with an "apprentice leader;" and how to find creative ways to do group prayer. In addition, the book includes material and tips on handling potential conflict and difficult personalities, forming group covenants, inviting new members, improving listening skills, studying the Bible, and much more. Using *Leading Life-Changing Small Groups* will help you create a group that members love to be a part of.

Now let's discuss the different elements of this small group study guide and how to use them for the session portion of your group meeting.

THE BIG PICTURE

Each session will begin with a short story or overview of the lesson theme. This is called "The Big Picture" because it introduces the central theme of the session. You will need to read this section as a group or have group members read it on their own before discussion begins. Here are three ways you can approach this section of the small group session:

As the group leader, read this section out loud for the whole group and then move into the questions in the next section, "A Wide Angle View." (You might read the first week, but then use the other two options below to encourage group involvement.)

Ask a group member to volunteer to read this section for the group. This allows another group member to participate. It is best to ask someone in advance to give them time to read over the section before reading it to the group. It is also good to ask someone to volunteer, and not to assign this task. Some people do not feel comfortable reading in front of a group. After a group member has read this section out loud, move into the discussion questions.

Allow time at the beginning of the session for each person to read this section silently. If you do this, be sure to allow enough time for everyone to finish reading so they can think about what they've read and be ready for meaningful discussion.

A WIDE ANGLE VIEW

This section includes one or more questions that move the group into a general discussion of the session topic. These questions are designed to help group members begin discussing the topic in an open and honest manner. Once the topic of the lesson has been established, move on to the Bible passage for the session.

A BIBLICAL PORTRAIT

This portion of the session includes a Scripture reading and one or more questions that help group members see how the theme of the session is rooted and based in biblical teaching. The Scripture reading can be handled just like "The Big Picture" section: You can read it for the group, have a group member read it, or allow time for silent reading. Make sure everyone has a Bible or that you have Bibles available for those who need them. Once you have read the passage, ask the question(s) in this section so that group members can dig into the truth of the Bible.

SHARPENING THE FOCUS

The majority of the discussion questions for the session are in this section. These questions are practical and help group members apply biblical teaching to their daily lives.

SNAPSHOTS

The "Snapshots" in each session help prepare group members for discussion. These anecdotes give additional insight to the topic being discussed. Each "Snapshot" should be read at a designated point in the session. This is clearly marked in the session as well as in the Leader's Notes. Again, follow the same format as you do with "The Big Picture" section and the "Biblical Portrait" section: Either you read the anecdote, have a group member volunteer to read, or provide time for silent reading. However you approach this section, you will find these anecdotes very helpful in triggering lively dialogue and moving discussion in a meaningful direction.

PUTTING YOURSELF IN THE PICTURE

Here's where you roll up your sleeves and put the truth into action. This portion is very practical and action-oriented. At the end of each session there will be suggestions for one or two ways group members can put what they've just learned into practice. Review the action goals at the end of each session and challenge group members to work on one or more of them in the coming week.

You will find follow-up questions for the "Putting Yourself in the Picture" section at the beginning of the next week's session. Starting with the second week, there will be time set aside at the beginning of the session to look back and talk about how you have tried to apply God's Word in your life since your last time together.

PRAYER

You will want to open and close your small group with a time of prayer. Occasionally, there will be specific direction within a session for how you can do this. Most of the time, however, you will need to decide the best place to stop and pray. You may want to pray or have a group member volunteer to begin the lesson with a prayer. Or you might want to read "The Big Picture" and discuss the "Wide Angle View" questions before opening in prayer. In some cases, it might be best to open in prayer after you have read the Bible passage. You need to decide where you feel an opening prayer best fits for your group.

When opening in prayer, think in terms of the session theme and pray for group members (including yourself) to be responsive to the truth of Scripture and the working of the Holy Spirit. If you have seekers in your group (people investigating Christianity but not yet believers) be sensitive to your expectations for group prayer. Seekers may not yet be ready to take part in group prayer.

Be sure to close your group with a time of prayer as well. One option is for you to pray for the entire group. Or you might allow time for group members to offer audible prayers that others can agree with in their hearts. Another approach would be to allow a time of silence for one-on-one prayers with God and then to close this time with a simple "Amen."

OVERCOMING ADVERSITY

ISAIAH 43:1–3

INTRODUCTION

How does a nearly defeated person take courage? How does a discouraged person decide to resist defeat and learn to become an overcomer? How do we face adversity and learn to stand strong, even when the storms of life try to knock us down? In my own experience, it usually boils down to three things: 1) What you believe, 2) How you grieve, 3) And who you lean on. Adversity can cause spiritual vertigo. When we begin to lose our balance and direction, we need to get back to the basics. We must anchor ourselves on the truth of God's Word, be honest about the pain we are facing, and allow other Christ followers to support us through the hard times.

THE BIG PICTURE

Take time to read this introduction with the group. There are suggestions for how this can be done in the beginning of the leader's section.

A WIDE ANGLE VIEW

Question One We all face adversity in life. There is no shame in this fact and no reason to be embarrassed about it. Take time as a group to honestly tell the details of when you faced adversity and what helped you make it through this difficult time. If we can't admit our struggles, it will be impossible to overcome them.

A BIBLICAL PORTRAIT

Read Isaiah 43:1–3

Question Two Isaiah is clear that all of us will face trials, struggles, and adversities. This is part of walking through life. Too often we buy into the false idea that being a Christ follower guarantees a life with no pain. This is simply not true. We can also begin to feel that God has deserted us in the midst of the storm. This is also false thinking. Isaiah teaches us that adversity will come, but God will never leave us alone or let the struggles of life overcome us. He offers us power to overcome adversity.

Question Three Take time as a group to identify the adversities you are facing right now in your life. As a leader, encourage people to focus on present adversity and not on something they overcame years ago.

SHARPENING THE FOCUS

Read Snapshot "What You Believe" before Question 4

Questions Four & Five God is not the author of evil! Jesus taught that there are two forces at work in this world: the Evil One and God the Father. He said the Evil One comes to steal, destroy, and kill. That is his nature, his agenda, and what he seeks to do in this world. Jesus also taught that His Father came to give life in all of its fullness.

When things are stolen, when a destructive power creates havoc in your life, when you stand at the coffin of a sixteen-year-old boy hit by a drunken driver, don't start blaming God. When you hear horror stories of hatred, oppression, prejudice, greed, and abuse, don't go knocking on God's door. These things are the work of the Enemy.

Conversely, when grace, forgiveness, kindness, and love come your way, know that God is at work! When someone offers you a second chance, blesses your life, encourages you or serves you, be confident that God is in it. Jesus came to give life, encouragement, grace, salvation, and a new beginning.

God limits the severity of what we suffer. He makes sure that only a certain amount of adversity comes, and He provides power for you to overcome it. God will never allow you to be swept away by adversity. Hang on to this truth with all your strength when things get hard in your life. Reflect on verses like 1 John 4:4: "You, dear children, are from God and have overcome them, because the one who is in you is greater than the one who is in the world," and Philippians 4:13: "I can do everything through him who gives me strength."

God is completely available in the middle of our troubles. Psalm 34:18 reminds us that "The LORD is close to the brokenhearted and saves those who are crushed in spirit." Psalm 23 tells us that although we might walk through the valley of the shadow of death, we will never be alone. God is with us in the middle of the darkest night. We can talk to Him, He listens to us, He understands, and He cares. This knowledge often makes the difference between caving in or taking courage, giving up or trusting.

God is committed to bringing good out of the hardships of our lives. Romans 8:28 says, "And we know that in all things God works for the good of those who love him, who have been called according to his purpose." Sometimes all we can see in the heartbreaks of life is the pain and struggle. But God sees the refining process. He can use any and all adversities to bring about something good. This does not mean God causes all adversity. (Look again at the first paragraph of this leader's note.) But, God can bring good even out of the painful suffering that comes into this world through the Evil One.

Read Snapshot "How You Grieve" before Question 6

Question Six We all need examples of those who have gone through the grieving process and come out on the other side as overcomers. Take time as a group to tell your stories of God's strength in the midst of the grieving process.

Question Seven This question might be a little tougher. You may want to take a few moments for silent reflection and prayer. Ask group members to think deeply about an area of pain, struggle, or adversity that they are still harboring in their heart. Take time for members to communicate this struggle to the other group members, opening the door for the grieving process to begin. You may even want to pair up for this exercise.

Read Snapshot "Who You Lean On" before Question 8

Questions Eight & Nine God made us for community. We are strongest when we are surrounded by other followers of Christ and weakest when we try to face life alone. Take time as a group and identify how you can help each other through times of adversity. As you conclude your small group, be sure everyone knows that the invitation to tell each other about your struggles and adversity is always extended. Don't let this be a one-week focus and then close the door to support, care, and encouragement. Be sure you come back to this topic with group members often and invite them to communicate their struggles so that you can be God's overcoming community together.

Putting Yourself in the Picture

Let the group members know you will be providing time at the beginning of the next meeting for them to discuss how they have put their faith into action. Let them tell about how they have acted on one of the two options above. However, don't limit their interaction to these two options. They may have put themselves into the picture in some other way as a result of your study. Allow for honest and open communication.

Also, be clear that there will not be any kind of a "test" or forced reporting. All you are going to do is allow time for people to volunteer to talk about how they have applied what they learned in your last study. Some group members will feel pressured if they think you are going to make everyone report on how they acted on these action goals. You don't want anyone to skip the next group because they are afraid of having to say they did not follow up on what they learned from the prior session. The key is to provide a place for honest communication without creating pressure and fear of being embarrassed.

Every session from this point on will open with a look back at the "Putting Yourself in the Picture" section of the previous session.

OVERCOMING FEAR

PSALM 23 AND 2 TIMOTHY 1:7

INTRODUCTION

In this session we will focus on how we can overcome fear. It is important, however, to recognize that some fear should not be overcome. Constructive fear is helpful, and we should acknowledge it and learn from it. When you get a little anxious while driving on ice-slicked roads, your fear might just keep you out of a ditch. When you fret just a bit over a huge presentation at work or a big exam you are taking, your fear can keep you alert and realistic about the consequences of your actions. Fear can motivate us to fasten our seat belts, show up for work every day, or pay our taxes. Jesus, who often said, "Fear not," also said, "Be afraid of the One who can destroy both soul and body in hell" (Matt. 10:28). In other words, some fear is legitimate.

Our focus in this session will be on the fear that God wants us to overcome. When we talk about overcoming fear, some Bible teachers create a bit of a false impression. They say that God will take all your fear away. Just ask Him to and He will wave a spiritual wand and it will be gone. This is an overstatement. The Bible shows that overcoming fear is to be a joint venture; God will do His part, but we must join in the process. Pray for God to give you courage as you prepare to face fear and discover the power to overcome!

THE BIG PICTURE

Take time to read this introduction with the group. There are suggestions for how this can be done in the beginning of the leader's section.

A WIDE ANGLE VIEW

Question One Provide time for group members to tell their stories of facing moments of fear. Everyone has had moments when they have felt intense fear of one sort or another.

A BIBLICAL PORTRAIT

Read Psalm 23 and 2 Timothy 1:7

Question Two Psalm 23 is one of the most familiar passages in the Bible. It paints the picture of a shepherd who loves, leads, and protects his sheep. It is a picture of God and His people. Often we think of this passage as a text for funerals. While it is certainly deeply meaningful at that time, it is really given as a word of encouragement for the living. When we fear, when we are anxious, when we feel our future is uncertain, we need to remember the messages of this psalm. Read this psalm as if you were a person in the middle of a fearful situation. What kind of hope and encouragement does it bring? Look closely at the character of the shepherd as well as the words of promise to those who are living with fear.

SHARPENING THE FOCUS

Read Snapshot "Understanding the Origins of Our Fear" before Question 4

Question Four There are many fears and a multitude of reasons these fears begin. I know people who will no longer drive because they put a car in a ditch thirty years ago. There are people who will not pursue deep relationships with anyone because they are afraid such relationships will only produce heartache, as they did twenty years ago. And there are people who stay away from God and the church because someone intimidated them spiritually when they were young. Take time as a group to identify some common fears and where these fears might begin.

When we peel back the layers of destructive fear, often the core of it all is found in just one or two events. The events themselves may not have been all that terrifying, but they were just scary enough to start tripping the dominoes. Once the avoidance pattern started, the fear just kept getting bigger and bigger. When we don't face it, fear escalates over time.

Question Five You have discussed fears in general. You have reflected on some of the source experiences that might have led to those fears. Take time now to go a little deeper. Focus on individual fears, past or present. Take time to dig into the history of where these fears were born.

Read Snapshot "Exposing the Lies" before Question 6

Questions Six & Seven Much of our fear is based on creative and sinister lies told by the Enemy. We begin to spin out unrealistic scenarios in our mind because the Enemy whisper deceit in our ears. One of the best ways to uncover the lies of the Enemy is to develop a practice of speaking the lie out loud Take time as a group to do this. Discuss some of the common lies that might come when you face the situations listed in question six. Work as a group to uncover some of the tactics of the devil in the example scenarios and then move to reflect together on real life situations your group members are facing

Read Snapshot "Declaring the Truth" before Question

Question Eight Fear thrives on deceit and its fire is fanned by the Evil One. Those of us who want to overcome the power of fear must expose its lies and diffuse the strength of those lies by speaking truthful words. Psalm 15:2 says we have to learn to speak the truth in our hearts. We must habitually speak the truth to ourselves and to others. It is a skill and it needs to be practiced. It is a discipline. We have to work at it. The power of God's truth always defeats the power of the Enemy's deceit. Truth will prevail. Close your group by speaking the truth to each other. You have spent time identifying the lies. Now boldly speak the truth of God to each other.

PUTTING YOURSELF IN THE PICTURE

Challenge group members to take time in the coming week to use part or all of this application section as an opportunity for continued growth.

OVERCOMING APATHY

LUKE 10:25—37

INTRODUCTION

This session focuses on overcoming apathy. We may not want to admit it, but this topic affects all of us. There is an internal pull toward a self-centered, apathetic, unconcerned lifestyle that touches each of us. In the story of the Good Samaritan we see two veteran religious leaders walk past a person in obvious need. They seem to have cold hearts, cloudy minds, and a frightening ability to keep their hands in their pockets. Jesus reminds us that it is quite possible to be very religious and yet devoid of even normal levels of human compassion.

Jesus pulls the veil back on a nasty little secret that lots of people don't want to discuss. Here it is: Much that goes on in the name of Jesus Christ has very little to do with Him at all. There are a lot of folks who do religion for reasons that have very little to do with the person of Jesus Christ and the love of Jesus Christ. Some people do religion for self-righteous reasons. Some do religion for power and control issues. Still others do religion in an attempt to get rid of guilt and shame. The point Jesus is really making, as He tells the story of the Good Samaritan, is that for a heart to be deeply touched by human suffering, it must first be opened up and filled with the love of Christ. When this happens, the frost of apathy begins to melt and the process of overcoming begins.

THE BIG PICTURE

Take time to read this introduction with the group. There are suggestions for how this can be done in the beginning of the leader's section.

A WIDE ANGLE VIEW

Question One We have all lived on both sides of the apathy issue. We have experienced times of deep concern and tangible efforts to make a difference. We have also felt cynicism and looked at situations through the lenses of apathy and disillusionment. Take time as a group to reflect on when you have felt great commitment to make a difference and also when you have felt apathetic toward situations around you.

A BIBLICAL PORTRAIT

Read Luke 10:25–37

Questions Two & Three This passage relates one of Jesus' most memorable parables. It is a story of a Jewish traveler who is traveling inside Jewish territory when he gets mugged beaten, robbed, and left half-dead along the side of a well-traveled road. A celebrated religious leader is about a half-mile away, walking toward the beaten and bloodied traveler. This would seem like good news! Help is on the way! But we know what happens next. The prominent religious leader veers about five degrees off the path so that he doesn't have to get too close to the wounded traveler. With an apathetic heart, he walks around the accident scene and keeps moving down the road.

The situation is only compounded when another key religious leader from the community does the same thing! The crowd listening to the story must have been shocked and amazed. Is there no one who cares about this beaten traveler?

Jesus tells about one more traveler who approaches the scene. He is a bit of a long shot because he is a Samaritan. This was an ethnic group that was hated by the Jews. The Samaritans were half-breeds. They had Jewish blood running through their veins, but it was tainted by intermarriage with people of pagan nations. But the Samaritan stops. He helps. He offers his resources. He models care and concern. He has discovered the antidote to apathy!

This story contrasts vivid pictures of apathy with those of compassion. Dig into the passage and unpack these contrasts.

SHARPENING THE FOCUS

Read Snapshot "Using Your Heart" before Question 4

Questions Four & Five Some of us have hearts that are working fine, but we fall back into apathy once in a while because of the sheer magnitude of the problems in our world. The statistics short-circuit our brains. We look at pictures of millions of starving people and feel our measly twenty dollars of discretionary money won't make a difference. We need to et the Holy Spirit soften our heart and help us feel for the needs of others. We need to allow our hearts to be broken for others. This is the beginning of overcoming apathy.

Read Snapshot "Using Your Head" before Question 6

Questions Six & Seven It takes mental discipline and intellectual tenacity to remember that assistance to one person can change the whole world for that one person. We must remind ourselves, "I don't have to change the whole world, but I can help one person. I can have an impact on one situation. I can make a life-changing difference in one life at a time."

Take time as a group to reflect on how you can make a difference through the combined effort and resources of your church and your small group. Use your intellect to strategize the best possible ways to implement your compassion in practical ways.

Read Snapshot "Using Your Hands" before Question 8

Questions Eight & Nine In the parable, the Good Samaritan did at least two things with his hands: He bandaged up the wounds of the victim and he wrote a blank check. Both of these things were critically important. When we get our hands dirty—when we are actually physically involved—we deal a death blow to apathy. It is difficult to remain hard-hearted when we are digging a hole for a Habitat home, swinging a hammer, using a shovel, feeding the hungry, helping the hurting, bandaging someone's wounds, using our financial means to assist, or living in the trenches with those in need. Take time to reflect on what might be keeping you from taking action to help others. Also, get practical about where you sense God is calling you to put your hands to work in the lives of those in need.

PUTTING YOURSELF IN THE PICTURE

Challenge group members to take time in the coming week to use part or all of this application section as an opportunity for continued growth.

OVERCOMING GREED

LUKE 18:18—30

INTRODUCTION

Addressing the topic of overcoming greed is touchy because greed is one of the most socially acceptable sins in our culture. In fact, there are so many manifestations of acceptable greed that we have begun to think it is normal. In our culture, if a person starts a business, pounds his employees mercilessly, undermines his competitors deceitfully, overcharges his customers regularly, but makes a fortune in the process, what do we call him or her? A success! We see the person ascend the *Forbes* ladder, watching him or her become an economic celebrity. It may never even cross our minds that maybe a lot of what is fueling this person's rocket is something the Bible calls greed.

The Bible calls us to be on our guard for any form of greed. Greed is not only an affliction of the affluent. Some of the greediest people on earth are those who have very few material possessions but who spend endless hours scheming, fantasizing, and standing in lottery lines, fully convinced that more money would solve every problem in their life. Greed motivates us to try to earn more than we need, own more than we can use, and to ache for stuff that, in reality, we have a sense will not even satisfy. It causes us to overwork, overspend, and overrule our most deeply held convictions.

THE BIG PICTURE

Take time to read this introduction with the group. There are suggestions for how this can be done in the beginning of the leader's section.

A WIDE ANGLE VIEW

Question One "Price Tag Moments" don't just happen in shopping malls; we face them in the rough and tumble moments of everyday life. Some years ago a survey was done y a group to find out what the average American would be willing to do in exchange for ten million dollars. Twenty-five percent said they would be willing to abandon their families. Twenty-three percent said they would become a prostitute for a week. Sixteen percent would leave their spouse. Three percent would put their kids up for adoption. When these people faced their hypothetical price tag moment, they did the mental, moral, and the economic math and allowed greed to undermine their deepest values.

A BIBLICAL PORTRAIT

Read Luke 18:18–30

Questions Two & Three This passage tells the story of an influential and quite affluent young guy who approached Jesus and asked how he could obtain eternal life. The young man has already achieved fortune and status. He has all he could ever want in this world, so why not start investing in the world to come?

Jesus sizes up this Wall-Street type and realizes the man is looking to make another big transaction—he's trying to make a deal with Jesus for heaven. Jesus first addresses the commands of God. He says, "Well, for starters I hope you have mastered the ten commandments perfectly. No lying, no stealing, no adultery, no dishonoring your parents. . . . " The young man breaks into a self-assured smile and sort of winks at Jesus and says, "Done that! Next." Jesus raises His eyebrows a bit and says, "Done that? No kidding? Perfectly? All ten?" The cocky young guy says, "All ten." Then he adds, "Since I was a youth."

The young man continues, saying, "What else do I have to do to gain eternal life?" Jesus responds, "Just one more thing. Sell your possessions, give the proceeds to the poor, and come and join Me." The color drains from this guy's face. He's just been hit by an eternal price tag moment.

Then the rich young ruler says in a low, firm voice, "No deal. It is not worth it to me." He slides back from the table, gets up and walks away. At this point Jesus said, just loudly enough for his twelve disciples to overhear, "It is very difficult for wealthy folks to enter into the kingdom of heaven."

You see, Jesus' carefully crafted challenge cut the rich young ruler's heart wide open for everybody to see. Greed and wealth had taken center stage. Long ago in this young guy's life there had been an exchange. God was not, in fact, the unquestioned leader of this young man's life—the love of money reigned supreme in his heart.

With this parable Jesus was not setting a precedent for all people in all places to give up all their earthly goods if they were going to follow Him. He was simply revealing a false god in this man's life and seeking to cast it off the throne. But the claws of riches and greed were so deep into this man's heart that he kept his money and walked away from Jesus.

Sharpening the Focus

Read Snapshot "Acknowledging the Reality of Greed" before Question 4

Questions Four & Five This is where the rubber hits the road. Take time as a group to rejoice in victories won against greed. Let these stories of overcoming stir your heart and deepen your faith as you commit to breaking the back of greed in your life. Also, invite your group members to enter this area of each other's life as prayer support and counselors. Let God give them perspective through others' wisdom and words.

Read Snapshot "Exposing Greed's Lies" before Question 6

Questions Six & Seven Both of these questions attack the lies that greed tells us. From our earliest days we hear the lies: If only I had a new bike, a new toy, the newest clothes, or whatever is in style, then I would be happy. As we grow, the list of toys and things change, but the sickness is the same. The lies grow more sophisticated and subtle, but they are still lies. Take time as a group to strip away the lies that the Enemy uses to bait us into a life of greed. Be very specific and direct. Some answers might be hypothetical and others may come right out of your group's life experience.

Read Snapshot "God's Program For Overcoming Greed" before Question 8

Questions Eight & Nine God has given a program for breaking the power of greed in our lives. Although we will all face the seduction of greed for our entire lives, there are weapons we can use in the battle to overcome it! Discuss the guideline that you find is strongest in your life. Your testimony of how you are growing in this area will be an encouragement and example to your group members. Also, humbly disclose where you struggle most. Invite your group members to support you and keep you accountable as you seek to grow in this area. We need each other if we are going to see radical transformation in this area of our life!

PUTTING YOURSELF IN THE PICTURE

Challenge group members to take time in the coming week to use part or all of this application section as an opportunity for continued growth.

OVERCOMING LUST

MATTHEW 5:27–30

INTRODUCTION

I know Christ followers today who would say, "Heaven should sing the Hallelujah chorus if I maintain physical purity in a world like this. Asking for a stain-free thought life is just asking too much. It is unrealistic." Others would say it is just impossible.

In this session we are going to focus on a subject matter that doesn't get much press. We are going to talk about lust. First, I am going to define what it really is, and then I am going to explain why it is so destructive. We are going to learn about the various levels of lusting and then we will dig into how we can overcome lust in the power of God. This is a sensitive subject and the questions have been designed to move you toward deep and meaningful interaction. At the same time, they are worded so that you can have good discussion without creating defensiveness. Because this is a topic we rarely talk about, please be prayerful concerning the tone and spirit of your group.

THE BIG PICTURE

The introduction to this session is going to be a bit different. The members of your small group are going to join in, using their imaginations. Ask a group member to read the introduction while the other group members close their eyes and listen.

A WIDE ANGLE VIEW

Question One God has given us the gift of imagination. It is wonderful and powerful. Tell your group members about some of the vivid images, feelings, and memories that flooded your mind as you read (or as someone else reads) the "Big Picture" section.

A Biblical Portrait

Read Matthew 5:27–30

Question Two We can imagine events and activities that are God-honoring and life-giving. We can also imagine events and activities that are destructive, cruel, and sinful. Nowhere does this come into sharper focus than when we link our powers to imagine with the highly combustible nature of our human sexuality. Jesus spoke directly to this matter in our passage from the Sermon on the Mount.

What is Jesus trying to say in this passage? He is speaking to a group of people who consider themselves to be very moral and virtuous folks. He is saying that before people pat themselves on the back for never sleeping in the wrong bed, they had better come to grips with whether or not they have been in the wrong bed in their minds. Jesus is saying there is more to sexual purity than mere external compliance. He is asking all of His followers to be every bit as sexually clean in their minds as they are with their bodies.

Question Three Jesus is not commanding His people to begin plucking out their eyes and chopping off their hands. These hyperbolic statements are meant to open our eyes to the seriousness of lust and to tie our hands, if that is what it takes, to keep them from acting on lustful desires. Jesus wants us to know that lust, and all the damage it brings, is serious business.

If there was ever a culture that needed to recapture an understanding of the seriousness of lust, it is ours! We have lost all sense of just how destructive lustful behaviors can be. We have given a cultural approval to lust-producing media, sanctioning it under "freedom of speech." Jesus speaks in the strongest terms possible because He knows the danger of lust and the consequences on spouses, children, health, happiness, and faith.

Sharpening the Focus

Read Snapshot "Two Foundational Questions" before Question 4

Questions Four & Five When you read the letter from a man trapped in the destructive cycle of lust, does he sound happy to you? Does he sound like someone who is doing some innocent thing that is not taking a toll of any kind? Does he sound like someone who is enjoying a sport? Does this seem like harmless play with no victims?

Once, when I taught on this topic, I received another unsolicited letter. This person wrote:

> Lust characterized my life. First, escape through fantasy. I tried to anesthetize the pain of my life with increasing doses of sexual thrills. Second, isolation. I withdrew from everybody and became lost in my own thoughts and hid from others to avoid exposure. Third, compulsiveness. I acted out sexually, ate food, and spent money uncontrollably. Fourth, fear and paranoia. I lived in terror that I would be caught and lose everything. Fifth, dishonesty. I deliberately and habitually lied about my actions and my whereabouts. Sixth, depression and despair. I spent all my physical and emotional energy on lust, growing increasingly weary from guilt. Seventh, resentment. I started to transfer my anger and guilt onto other people, and I even started to blame them for my need to act out. Eighth, an effort to do good religious works. I tried to compensate for my sin by doing good works for God, and it just never seemed enough.

People who get caught up in lust watch their life unravel a little bit at a time. It is not just the person caught up in lust that suffers, but the others around them. A woman wrote me a note communicating the pain that this topic had brought to her.

> On the sidelines are victims like me, women who question their own attractiveness and value because the one they love chooses to share the most intimate part of themselves with a paper fantasy. When they do share intimately with their marriage partner, it is tainted by the messages of pornography. It is usually an act of selfishness rather than an act of beauty and the oneness God designed it to be. You see, I know what it is like to live with someone whose mind has been poisoned by pornography.

Let's agree to be honest about this topic. No more lying to ourselves and others with lines like, "It is a victimless activity," "What she doesn't know won't hurt her," or "It is all innocent fun." It is time to begin acknowledging that lust hurts everyone.

Read Snapshot "Levels of Lusting" before Question 6

Question Six Lust, when left unchecked, will increase over time, not decrease. That is the secret power of lust: it is progressive. You start out at level one, and if you don't check it, counteract it, overcome it, you will eventually fall into level-two lust. If you don't take some action there, you will wind up in level-three lust. From there you are just awaiting the rash. What satisfies today won't satisfy tomorrow. What excites and provides the buzz today won't do it tomorrow. There is an ever-increasing pull into a secret world that gets darker and darker.

Our culture, with easy access to movies, magazines, the Internet, 1-900 phone numbers, and countless other lust-producing sources, is saturated with fuel for the fires of lust. Take time as a group to identify some of the primary sources of lust. Be very specific. Sometimes saying it out loud begins to pull back the veil and expose the source of the problem.

Question Seven This question is not meant to say there are not many similarities between men and women. We can't overgeneralize here, but there are some basic differences that most men and women can identify. What is lust-producing for men, is often not for women. For many men, visual images add fuel to the fire of lust; for many woman, it is images of romantic involvement in movies and books. For men, lust often tends to be a greater struggle than it does for women. Take time as a group to identify some of the differences between men and women when it comes to lusting.

Read Snapshot "Instructions for Overcoming Lust" before Question 8

Question Eight Take time to speak God's words of truth and grace to each other. Work as a group to overturn the lies the Enemy tells those who are battling lust. We all need to be reminded of God's love and care. Use this opportunity to reflect deeply on God's truth.

Question Nine None of us can walk through this life alone and remain strong and healthy. We need the strength and support we can draw from each other. Identify how you can become a support group for those dealing with lust as well as any other struggle.

PUTTING YOURSELF IN THE PICTURE

Challenge group members to take time in the coming week to use part or all of this application section as an opportunity for continued growth.

OVERCOMING SORROW

JOHN 11:32–44 AND PSALM 116:1–9

INTRODUCTION

One hard reality we will all face in life is sorrow. The holidays might intensify these feelings, but they can hit us any time of the year. Loss of a loved one, a broken friendship, health problems, an uncertain future, and losing a job are just a few of the possible sources of sorrow.

When loss comes our way, often we wish we could take a month or two off from life and find a quiet place to heal. The reality is, most of us still have to press on with our daily life. We have to get up in the morning, put our clothes on, go to work, eat meals, relate to people, care for those we love, and find a way to fall asleep at the end of the day. Then, we have get up and do it again the next day. Thankfully, God has given us some tools for living with sorrow and walking through it in His power. There is hope in Christ for overcoming sorrow!

THE BIG PICTURE

Take time to read this introduction with the group. There are suggestions for how this can be done in the beginning of the leader's section.

A WIDE ANGLE VIEW

Question One Johnny, in the "Big Picture" story, learned the conventional wisdom on this topic. He learned that the way to manage sorrow is to bury your feelings, replace your loss as soon as possible, grieve alone, allow time to heal all things, live with regret, and not get too close to people or you will get burned again. Have group members reflect on what kind of messages they received growing up about how to manage sorrow.

BIBLICAL PORTRAIT

Read John 11:32–44 and Psalm 116:1–9

Question Two Jesus was perfect. Although divine, He embodied all that it meant to be perfect as a person. With this in mind, we see Him express a depth of care and a freedom to express His sorrow. He did not bottle up His pain. He did not live by the lies, "Real men don't cry," or "Handle your pain in private." He wept openly and invited others into His sorrow. What an example for those of us who want to be more like our Savior.

Question Three The psalmist did a number of things in the midst of his sorrow: (1) He cried out to God. Instead of blaming God or running away, He cried out to the One who could help him; (2) he realized that God heard him. This led to a deeper commitment to follow God; (3) he praised God and reflected deeply on God's character. His lips were filled with words such as "gracious," "righteous," and "compassionate." In the midst of his sorrow, the psalmist knew that the character of God did not change; and (4) he declared that God was the One who delivers. In the darkness of sorrow, this man discovered that salvation comes only from God.

SHARPENING THE FOCUS

Read Snapshot "Conventional Wisdom on Sorrow Management" before Question 4

Question Four When I was doing some research on grief management I found that there are a lot of grief-laden people who follow the conventional wisdom on this topic. Sadly, they often wind up in ditches of alcoholism, drug abuse, workaholism, broken relationships, and compulsive eating and spending patterns, all driven by an inability to recover and rebuild their lives after incurring a devastating loss.

The message to me and to you should be loud and clear. If you grieve right, you can live right afterwards; if you grieve wrong, all bets are off. Before we can look at healthy grief management, we need to uncover the deceit of the conventional wisdom on this topic. If we buy the party line, we will continue to hit roadblocks.

As you look at the conventional wisdom's six elements of grief management, clarify how each one can actually do more damage than good. Even if it is an approach you have used, be honest about how it can (and maybe has) hurt the process of healing.

Questions Five & Six Take time as a group to counteract some of the false beliefs about sorrow and grieving. Use the scenario to make it practical. Identify how you would counter the negative and unhealthy statements about the grief process. Next, let the focus move to your own life. Identify unhealthy patterns and invite group members to pray and support you in your effort to overcome sorrow in your life from a Christ-honoring perspective.

Read Snapshot "God's Wisdom on Sorrow Management" before Question 7

Question Seven God's plan for sorrow management is diametrically opposed to conventional wisdom. Set each element of conventional wisdom about sorrow management up against God's wisdom. They correspond number for number. The first element of the conventional wisdom is the opposite of the first element of God's plan for overcoming sorrow. Look at the contrasts and see how God's plan is radically different than the wisdom of the world.

Question Eight Close your group with a time of prayer and encouragement. Commit to support each other through your times of sorrow. Open the door for this to happen now, and any time your group gathers. Agree that no one in your group will come and go from your gathering without inviting the others to help carry the burden of their sorrow.

PUTTING YOURSELF IN THE PICTURE

Challenge group members to take time in the coming week to use part or all of this application section as an opportunity for continued growth.

ADDITIONAL WILLOW CREEK RESOURCES

Small Group Resources

Coaching Life-Changing Small Group Leaders, by Bill Donahue and Greg Bowman
The Complete Book of Questions, by Garry Poole
The Connecting Church, by Randy Frazee
Leading Life-Changing Small Groups, by Bill Donahue and the Willow Creek Team
The Seven Deadly Sins of Small Group Ministry, by Bill Donahue and Russ Robinson
Walking the Small Group Tightrope, by Bill Donahue and Russ Robinson

Evangelism Resources

Becoming a Contagious Christian (book), by Bill Hybels and Mark Mittelberg
The Case for a Creator, by Lee Strobel
The Case for Christ, by Lee Strobel
The Case for Faith, by Lee Strobel
Seeker Small Groups, by Garry Poole
The Three Habits of Highly Contagious Christians, by Garry Poole

Spiritual Gifts and Ministry

Network Revised (training course), by Bruce Bugbee and Don Cousins
The Volunteer Revolution, by Bill Hybels
What You Do Best in the Body of Christ—Revised, by Bruce Bugbee

Marriage and Parenting

Fit to Be Tied, by Bill and Lynne Hybels
Surviving a Spiritual Mismatch in Marriage, by Lee and Leslie Strobel

Ministry Resources

An Hour on Sunday, by Nancy Beach
Building a Church of Small Groups, by Bill Donahue and Russ Robinson
The Heart of the Artist, by Rory Noland
Making Your Children's Ministry the Best Hour of Every Kid's Week, by Sue Miller and
    David Staal
Thriving as an Artist in the Church, by Rory Noland

Curriculum

An Ordinary Day with Jesus, by John Ortberg and Ruth Haley Barton
Becoming a Contagious Christian (kit), by Mark Mittelberg, Lee Strobel, and Bill Hybels
Good Sense Budget Course, by Dick Towner, John Tofilon, and the Willow Creek Team
If You Want to Walk on Water, You've Got to Get Out of the Boat, by John Ortberg with
    Stephen and Amanda Sorenson
The Life You've Always Wanted, by John Ortberg with Stephen and Amanda Sorenson
The Old Testament Challenge, by John Ortberg with Kevin and Sherry Harney, Mindy
    Caliguire, and Judson Poling

Willow Creek Association
Vision, Training, Resources for Prevailing Churches

This resource was created to serve you and to help you build a local church that prevails. It is just one of many ministry tools that are part of the Willow Creek Resources® line, published by the Willow Creek Association together with Zondervan.

The Willow Creek Association (WCA) was created in 1992 to serve a rapidly growing number of churches from across the denominational spectrum that are committed to helping unchurched people become fully devoted followers of Christ. Membership in the WCA now numbers over 10,500 Member Churches worldwide from more than ninety denominations.

The Willow Creek Association links like-minded Christian leaders with each other and with strategic vision, training, and resources in order to help them build prevailing churches designed to reach their redemptive potential. Here are some of the ways the WCA does that.

- **A2: Building Prevailing Acts 2 Churches—Today**—an annual two-and-a-half day event, held at Willow Creek Community Church in South Barrington, Illinois, to explore strategies for building churches that reach out to seekers and build believers, and to discover new innovations and breakthroughs from Acts 2 churches around the country.

- **The Leadership Summit**—a once a year, two-and-a-half-day conference to envision and equip Christians with leadership gifts and responsibilities. Presented live at Willow Creek as well as via satellite broadcast to over one hundred locations across North America, this event is designed to increase the leadership effectiveness of pastors, ministry staff, volunteer church leaders, and Christians in the marketplace.

- **Ministry-Specific Conferences**—throughout each year the WCA hosts a variety of conferences and training events—both at Willow Creek's main campus and offsite, across the U.S., and around the world—targeting church leaders and volunteers in ministry-specific areas such as: evangelism, small groups, preaching and teaching, the arts, children, students, women, volunteers, stewardship, raising up resources, etc.

- **Willow Creek Resources®**—provides churches with trusted and field-tested ministry resources in such areas as leadership, evangelism, spiritual formation, spiritual gifts, small groups, stewardship, student ministry, children's ministry, the use of the arts-drama, media, contemporary music —and more.

- **WCA Member Benefits**—includes substantial discounts to WCA training events, a 20 percent discount on all Willow Creek Resources®, *Defining Moments* monthly audio journal for leaders, quarterly *Willow* magazine, access to a Members-Only section on WillowNet, monthly communications, and more. Member Churches also receive special discounts and premier services through WCA's growing number of ministry partners—Select Service Providers—and save an average of $500 annually depending on the level of engagement.

For specific information about WCA conferences, resources, membership, and other ministry services contact:

Willow Creek Association
P.O. Box 3188
Barrington, IL 60011-3188
Phone: 847-570-9812
Fax: 847-765-5046
www.willowcreek.com

TOUGH QUESTIONS

Garry Poole and Judson Poling

Softcover

How Does Anyone Know God Exists?	ISBN 0-310-24502-8
What Difference Does Jesus Make?	ISBN 0-310-24503-6
How Reliable Is the Bible?	ISBN 0-310-24504-4
How Could God Allow Suffering and Evil?	ISBN 0-310-24505-2
Don't All Religions Lead to God?	ISBN 0-310-24506-0
Do Science and the Bible Conflict?	ISBN 0-310-24507-9
Why Become a Christian?	ISBN 0-310-24508-7
Leader's Guide	ISBN 0-310-24509-5

REALITY CHECK SERIES

by Mark Ashton

Winning at Life	ISBN: 0-310-24525-7
Leadership Jesus Style	ISBN: 0-310-24526-5
When Tragedy Strikes	ISBN: 0-310-24524-9
Sudden Impact	ISBN: 0-310-24522-2
Jesus' Greatest Moments	ISBN: 0-310-24528-1
Hot Issues	ISBN: 0-310-24523-0
Future Shock	ISBN: 0-310-24527-3
Clear Evidence	ISBN: 0-310-24746-2

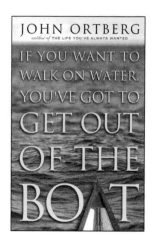

We want to hear from you. Please send your comments about this book to us in care of zreview@zondervan.com. Thank you.

GRAND RAPIDS, MICHIGAN 49530 USA

WWW.ZONDERVAN.COM